The Art of Just Being … ME!

An Interactive Guide to Finding the Courage to Just Be You

MYLIRA GREEN

Copyright © 2017 M. Green Enterprises, LLC.

All rights reserved.

ISBN: 1537593633
ISBN-13: 978-1537593630

DEDICATION

I dedicate this book to my two children I never was granted the opportunity to meet. Because your spirits never became flesh, I took my spirit more seriously and discovered the real me the world needed to see. Mommy loves you both.

CONTENTS

Acknowledgments

1 Introduction

2 Acknowledge the Truth

3 Embrace Your Differences

4 Utilize Your Strengths

5 Embrace Your Weaknesses

6 Become Comfortable with the Real You

About the Author

ACKNOWLEDGMENTS

I would like to thank my husband for serving as my balance and encouraging me to go after my hopes, dreams, and desires. I would also like to acknowledge the spirit of my daughter, which revealed to me the importance of leaving a legacy. This resulted in the courage to finally put my thoughts in a book. Lastly, I am grateful to my family and friends who supported me during this period of building a legacy for my daughter.

I would also like to say a special thank you to those individuals who assisted with making this dream a reality. Thank you Angie Kiesling of The Editorial Attic and editor Kathy Curtis for editing my book. Also, thank you Katheryn Watkins of Kat and Company Designs for putting my vision into a visual display on the cover of this book. Lastly, a special thank you goes to my aunt, Quniana Futrell of BRC Building Resilience in Communities and the ECE Firm, for providing consultation during this process. I really appreciate each of you ladies and thank you from the depths of my heart.

INTRODUCTION

The art of just being yourself may seem like something that should come naturally. Many spend a lifetime chasing after what those around them have or say they should have. This pursuit of false identity leads to a never-ending cycle of chasing a fabricated reality. However, there is hope. Learning the art of just being yourself will end this cycle permanently and provide you with the platform to reach your goals, dreams, and life's desires.

Learning this art is imperative to your life because without this skill the world will miss out on your uniqueness. If the world does not have the opportunity to benefit from the real you, there will be a problem that will never receive a solution because you hold the key to that resolution. If you are comfortable in your own skin, it frees you and provides generations after you an example of a victor and champion. This in turn will promote others to see the importance of being themselves.

For years I lived in a false reality and can attest that learning this skill provides a true sense of liberation. I dealt with depression, anxiety, suicide ideation, and even survived a suicide attempt. These mental and emotional stumbling blocks were the result of feeling I would never be good enough. I viewed myself as a victim of premature sexual activity, rape, and low self-esteem due to a corrupt self-body image.

When I walked in this false reality, anything other than the real me seemed to be a better option. I lived with multiple masks I chose from daily, depending on the occasion or the person I was speaking with at the time. I became Mylira the victim, Mylira the gossiper, Mylira the liar, Mylira the partier, Mylira the hypocrite, Mylira the fornicator, Mylira the pessimist, Mylira the attention seeker, Mylira the doubter, and Mylira the broken woman striving to meet the expectations of others.

Then one day I had an epiphany. I was spending all my time focusing on what happened to me and where I wanted to be and never took the time to live in the present. I decided to learn from my past and become the solution to a problem I saw in this world, people not being comfortable with their true selves. I had to admit my problem was not the world or those that hurt me, but was my never accepting the added value I brought to this world.

When I realized my worth, I was fortified to walk through the steps of learning the art of just being me. I acknowledged the truth, embraced my differences, utilized my strengths, accepted my weaknesses, and finally learned how to become comfortable with my real self. I was able to walk in a freedom I never experienced before. I no longer chased after what the world said I should be doing and started to be my honest self. Now I encourage others to do the same!

If you are ready to build the courage to be yourself, then get your notepad and pen ready. You are going to need them as you prepare to go on this journey of learning the art of just being ... you!

Before you get started, take some time to self-reflect by answering the following questions:

1) Why did you pick up this interactive guide to finding the courage to just be you?

   a) What about this book stood out to you?

b) What about the introduction encouraged you to continue on this journey?

2) What do you desire to gain from this interactive guide?

   a) Which aspect of the table of contents do you think will be the easiest for you to accomplish? Why?
   b) What do you think you may struggle with more? Why?

3) What hesitations do you currently have about becoming comfortable with the real you?

   a) What do you think you need to do to address these hesitations?
   b) What commitment do you need to make before becoming comfortable with the real you?

ACKNOWLEDGE THE TRUTH

Acknowledging the truth is the first step to gaining the courage to be yourself. You then learn why being you is imperative to your spiritual, mental, physical, emotional, and social health. This provides the call to action of recognizing that a change needs to happen to the change actually happening.

Well, what exactly is the truth? I am so glad you asked. The truth that needs to be acknowledged is that no two people were created the same. No two people were formed to think, feel, look, or react the same way. No two people were fashioned to experience or accomplish the same things or created with the same purpose. So why does it seem we chase what others have?

The way we think about ourselves stems from what we see and hear around us. Whether through the lives and experiences of our family members, stories and advice from our friends, or the images published in the media, our personal self-concept is wrapped in the images that are portrayed.

Our families want us to be better than the prior generation, so we chase a lifestyle that appears better. Our friends care about us so much that they tell us what we should do or should not do, so we listen. The media shows the image of a more slender and richer self, so we diet, exercise, and chase occupations or education that is supposed to guarantee a six-figure salary. However, there comes a time where these are not enough.

The truth is relevant to your becoming free to just be you. Once it is acknowledged, you won't feel as if you have to keep yourself in a box. This box may be family generational curses that you may have grown comfortable with living in.

For example, in my family, most women were prematurely introduced to sex and experienced molestation and rape. We unintentionally became comfortable in that place and created a relationship with fear. As a result, we did not talk about the abuse we experienced because we became used to the darkness in our "box" (life). At a young age we knew not to tell anyone what was going on in our family, no matter what negativity was in our minds and bodies due to emotional and physical abuse. The unfortunate reality was due to this comfort zone, which never skipped a generation.

Once I realized the core behind this misfortune, I was the first one in my family to verbalize what happened to me so the same thing would not happen to my daughter. When I broke my silence, it killed the excuses that were keeping my family's generational curses alive. I had to be honest with the things that happened in my life before I could even address who I really was during a specific phase of my life. Acknowledging this truth placed me outside the box, and resulted in my being the best me there was.

Embracing the truth of your reality liberates you, and this is why it is imperative to acknowledge your story as your own. Your story is meant to learn from and not to discourage you. When you are ashamed by your own story it becomes easy to exhibit someone else's story. This is detrimental to your becoming your true self.

The greatest gift you can give yourself when starting this journey is acknowledging that your journey is not supposed to look like someone else's journey. Your story is unique to you. Yes, you can learn from others and they can also learn from you, but your story is supposed to be a reflection of your own purpose. This truth serves as the cornerstone of growing comfortable with the real you!

Are you still wondering what your truth is? Answer the questions below in hopes to gain more clarity:

1) What is your understanding of the truth?

    a) Why do you believe this truth is imperative to your journey?

    b) How will you apply this truth during this process?

2) When was a time you ignored this truth?

    a) How did this impact how you felt about yourself?

    b) Did it have an impact on your actions? How?

3) What lies have you told yourself to ignore this truth?

    a) What truths will you implement now during this journey?

    b) Why do you believe doing this is important to your journey?

EMBRACE YOUR DIFFERENCES

After you acknowledge the truth that no two people are the same, embrace the attributes and experiences that make you different and add value to the world and those around you. It is easy to accept what seems normal to the masses. What makes you stand out from the crowd may make you feel like an outcast. If the majority looks different, you may shy away from your true dreams and purpose. However, I am here to tell you there is no value in suppressing the real you. The world is waiting on the real you to shine a light during a time that is filled with so much darkness.

You may be wondering right now, "Well, Mylira, what are my differences? I do not see the value that I bring to this world." I'm delighted you asked because I have an answer for you. Your differences are defined as the attributes you find yourself trying to run away from because of the fear of rejection and failure.

The dreams you keep holding off are the things that make you different. But that comes at a cost: You want to make sure your family is taken care of so you keep that nine-to-five job you do not even find pleasure in anymore. You want to comfortably retire one day, and starting a new career has the potential to fail. Maybe you do not want anyone to look at you like you are crazy because your ideas don't resemble the person they are familiar with.

Some of you may say, "I hear you, but there is no way a person with my past could ever succeed in anything this life has to offer." I am here to tell you to **GET OUT OF YOUR OWN WAY**! Your past is not a disqualifier, no matter how much you have been through or the mistakes you have made trying to figure out this thing called life. It just makes room to relate with others who may be trying to get through what you have already gotten through.

From the age of three to thirteen I battled with liking women, engaged in premature sexual activity until one day someone ignored my "no," and hated myself so much I did anything to fit in until one day I saw no need to be alive. If I had focused on my past I would not have been able to accomplish everything I have at the age of twenty-four. I am a wife and mother, a mastered level social worker, a supervisee in social work, business owner, certified life and career coach, and now a published columnist and author.

I did not allow my flaws and past to serve as a stumbling block but as a learning experience. I also learned I must be worth something because I made it through, so the same applies for you. Your coming out on the other side of your test should show you there is some power in you that brings out value worth living during this lifetime.

I know accepting what makes you different is easier said than done. However, embracing these things serves as the foundation of seeing your value. If you never see your value you may become complacent because you will become comfortable just existing and not living. As a result, you may never see a true reason to live other than reaching the milestones society says you should reach (i.e., college or the military, a good-paying job to become independent, the role of wife and mother without putting yourself first, etc.). This will keep you from embracing what makes you different, which may result in the world never benefiting from the beauty of you.

Now is the time to learn what makes you special. Karen Clarke Sheard stated in one of her songs "You gotta see it, before you see it, or you never will see it." You have to see yourself worthy enough to have value or you never will see the benefit you bring to this world. Your goals, dreams, and aspirations may be left unfulfilled and a problem in this world may be left without its proper solution, which is YOU!

Below are a few questions that may help you embrace your differences:

1) What are some things you have been "putting off"?

    a) Why have you put these things to the side?

    b) What would it take for you to pursue those things?

2) Sometimes our perception of the past can cripple us from moving forward. What is your story?

Be as honest and detailed as possible, even if it takes you multiple days or weeks to complete this question. You do not have to share this with anyone else. However, the more honest you are with yourself, the easier it will be to see how far you have come in your life.

    a) What part of your story stands out to you the most?

    b) What lesson can others learn from your experiences?

3) After reflecting on your story and acknowledging what you have been putting off, what are your differences?

If you find yourself still struggling with discovering what your differences are, it is okay to ask people you

***TRUST AND KNOW WILL ADD VALUE TO YOUR LIFE** what they feel makes you different. This may help give you some direction and serve as a foundation for you.*

a) What value do these differences bring to the world and those around you?

b) What would help you embrace these differences?

UTILIZE YOUR STRENGTHS

Embracing your differences is the catalyst for utilizing your strengths. This seems like rocket science. But if you live your life as society dictates, you do not utilize your strengths because it does not fit into what the majority is doing. Now that you know what makes you different, let's focus on your differences, identify your strengths, and help you to utilize them every day.

Your strengths go deeper than the things you can do well. They encompass your beliefs, values, and the ability to relate to others. When we were discussing what makes you different, I talked about the value you bring to this world. Utilizing your strengths helps you cultivate that value and touch the lives of others.

You may wonder if you have any strengths. The answer is simple; everyone does. You just have to know what to look for to determine what a strength is. Your strengths are those characteristics and gifts that come naturally to you. Your strengths bring you joy.

Why should your strengths bring you joy, you might ask? I am so glad you did! They should bring you joy because it is easier for you to utilize them. One of my strengths is encouraging others to see their own value. This brings me so much joy because I went through the steps (the ones in this interactive guide) to see my own value. Now in my career as a social worker and business owner I never feel like I am working but simply living, which has reportedly touched many lives.

Your strengths make a difference in the lives of others. I am not suggesting that you live to benefit others. However, every good thing bears good fruit. So you should be able to see some results from your strengths. Your strengths are tools you use to relate to others. These tools will help you discern how to interact with people and if what you are doing is aligned with your purpose.

Only you can determine how to implement your strengths. Your strengths are to assist you with reaching your goals, dreams, and aspirations. If not implemented correctly, you may return to being a people pleaser and putting yourself last. However, if you utilize your strengths to your advantage, the transformation from the woman who picked up this guide to the woman you want to be will go smoothly. This journey will no longer feel like a job. You will feel like yourself because you will be doing what comes naturally.

Do you need help determining your strengths? Then answer the questions below to assist in your discovery:

1) What things do you love to do?

   a) Do you see any results from implementing these things?

   b) If you do see results, what are they and what impact did they have on others? If you did not see results, why and what can you do differently?

2) After discovering what you love and what has produced the most fruit in your life, what would you say your strengths are?

   a) What strengths do you need to cultivate more, and how would this help bear more fruit in your life?

b) How would this help others?

3) Are you currently implementing your strengths in **ALL** areas of your life (i.e., spiritually, socially [including family and friends], and professionally)?

   a) If no, why not?

   b) What changes need to be made to ensure all areas of your life utilize your strengths?

EMBRACE YOUR WEAKNESSES

Please proceed with caution, for this may be the most difficult concept to grasp. It may be easy for you to embrace your strengths because they make you feel good and give you a sense of purpose. However, trying to embrace your weaknesses may lead you to feel a sense of inadequacy, so you may try to hide from them.

While hiding your weaknesses from others is an easy escape, embracing them is a beautiful thing, for no one is made without flaws. This concept may be new for many, so bear with me as I break down what I mean.

To embrace your weaknesses, you must admit they exist. No one likes to admit they have some flaws, but to ignore this reality opens yourself up to the inability to be humble. Humility is the catalyst for change. Nothing will change in your situation if you do not see there are things that need to be changed.

Once you admit your weaknesses, you will know where to start. This is why your transformation is necessary when learning the art of just being ... you. The biggest mistake people make when trying to cover their weaknesses is trying to do it themselves. This is where a good support system becomes imperative.

It is easier to work on yourself alone because no one can judge you. But when you allow your support system to cover your weaknesses until they become strengths, the stress and strain your transformation produces won't discourage you and knock you off your square. If not covered, you may throw in the towel and never become who you are striving to be.

Sometimes your weaknesses can be character based. They can also be time driven and may require asking for outside help. When my daughter was born I promised myself I was going to eat healthy. Every week I would buy fresh, healthy foods that I never cooked, and I threw away hundreds of dollars. In October of 2016, I found a plant-based meal prep program and decided to invest in it. Even though I meant well, adjusting to motherhood did not allow me to cook the way I wanted to. I utilized the meal prep program to cover my weakness of not having time.

To embrace your weaknesses you have to be honest with yourself and comfortable with depending on your support staff to help cover your weaknesses. This may be uncomfortable and take some time to implement, but once mastered, the support you receive will help keep you pressing towards your goals.

Now it's time for moments of honesty. Answer the questions below to help you become comfortable with embracing your weaknesses:

1) What are your weaknesses?

a) Do you think these weaknesses can change?

b) If so, how?

2) Going back to your list of weaknesses, who or what can help cover those weaknesses?

a) How comfortable are you getting those weaknesses covered by those individuals or things?

b) What would it take to actually ask for their help?

When you grow comfortable enough to ask for help, I suggest you discuss what you expect from those individuals to hold you accountable to this process.

3) How will covering your weaknesses help you during this journey of learning the art of just being you?

   a) Why do you believe this is important?

   b) Will you cover the weaknesses of others as well? Why or why not?

THE ART OF JUST BEING...ME!

BECOME COMFORTABLE WITH THE REAL YOU

Congratulations! You have made it to the last step!

Once you have acknowledged the truth, embraced your differences, utilized your strengths, and embraced your weaknesses, it is now time for you to become comfortable with just being you. It may seem easier to go back to doing what others expect from you, but the liberation that comes with learning the art of being you brings the joy you may have been missing.

Don't get discouraged if the process takes longer for you because everything takes trial and error. Seeing your value will help you keep pressing on when you feel like giving up.

Remember, being you has nothing to do with what others expect of you. You have **ALL** to do with what brings you the most peace and sense of accomplishment. Being comfortable only comes when you realize everyone is already taken, so the only person left to be is you.

It may be scary at first because you may feel people won't like the real you. I can't promise you won't feel lonely. However, I can promise once this art is mastered, you will feel more fulfilled!

Are you still feeling nervous about being the real you? Reflect on the questions below, with the hopes of feeling good in your own skin:

1) Thinking about what you have learned during this process, who are you?

    a) When you acknowledge the real you, what positive things do you add to the world and those around you?

    b) What do you still have to work on? How will you work on those things?

2) Are the hesitations you listed in the introduction still there?

    a) If they are, why? If not, why not?

    b) What would you tell someone who has reservations about discovering their true selves?

3) What can others learn from you after going through this journey?

    a) Would you recommend this book to someone else who is trying to find themselves?

    b) ***Please feel free to write a review about your journey on Amazon or email me at mgreenenterprisesllc@gmail.com with the subject: "Book Review". Thanks in advance!***

ABOUT THE AUTHOR

Mylira Green is the founder of M. Green Enterprises, LLC. She is an inspirational speaker, life skills workshop facilitator, published columnist and author, and career and life coach through a partnership with Sisters Helping Sisters in Business. Mylira is fiercely committed to guiding youth and young adults, ages thirteen through twenty-five, as well as women, to achieve their fullest potential so they can have the life and career of their dreams.

Mylira's path to becoming a professional speaker became clear at an early age. She was born in Norfolk, VA, but spent most of her childhood in the city of Suffolk. Here she experienced many childhood traumas that lead to a struggle with low self-esteem, depression, anxiety, and suicide ideations and attempts. At seventeen, she decided to take her life back to become the person she wished she had in her childhood, a social worker.

She graduated with a bachelor's of science in social work in 2013 from Norfolk State University and received a master's of social work with a clinical concentration in children and families from the University of Southern California in 2015. During her time at USC, she lost two children and almost gave up on her dream of being the social worker she worked so hard to be.

On May 5, 2016, she gave birth to her rainbow baby (a child born after losing two children to miscarriages). When she looked into her daughter's eyes, she realized she had to overcome her fears of failure and rejection to build a legacy her daughter would be proud to carry on. Now she is a mastered level social worker and supervisee in social work in the state of Virginia.

Her work is rewarding because people see they are worth pursuing. They are taught social life skills in a group setting, such as self-esteem, suicide prevention, sexuality, healthy relationships, etc. These people impact larger groups of individuals who in turn impact a larger scale of people. They change the future of today's generation and include those who attend the groups and conventions, family, friends, and community.

Mylira's personal and business strengths set her apart from other service providers. Her personal strength is seeing the good in everyone. She believes someone on the verge of giving up or losing everything can be encouraged to live life to the fullest. Her strength as a business owner is not having the mind for money but the mind for people. She has worked for many agencies where money came first, which quickly burned everyone out. Her passion of meeting the needs of people on a holistic scale makes her different from the masses.

Over the years, her expertise has been honored with remarkable and notable accolades, including the 2016 Triumphant Woman Award, and in the summer of 2016 she became an entrepreneur to build a legacy for her daughter. As a wife and a mother, she realized she had to become the solution to the problems she saw the youth, young adults, and women struggling with by becoming "the bridge between the caterpillar and butterfly." She strives to close the gap between a person's current reality and where they desire to be. She overcame her fears and built a testimony to help others overcome theirs and blossom into the butterflies they were created to be.

Made in the USA
Columbia, SC
18 April 2019